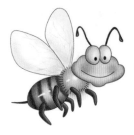

I CAN WRITE
WORDS

U0111295

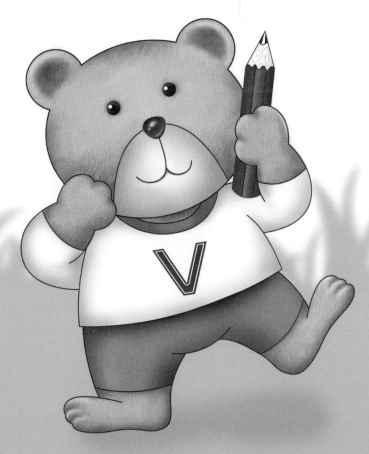

SUN YA PUBLICATIONS (HK) LTD.

www.sunya.com.hk

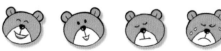

 A

 a

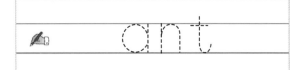 ant

ant

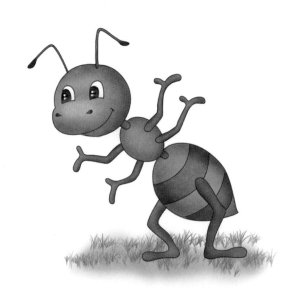

apple

apple

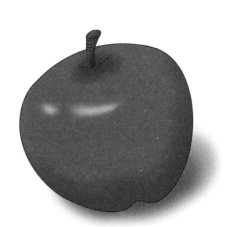

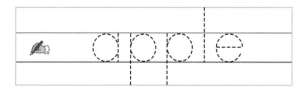

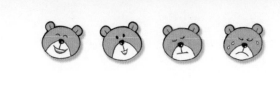

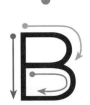

B

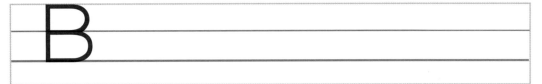

b

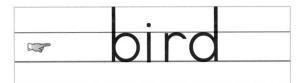
bird

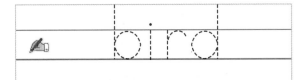

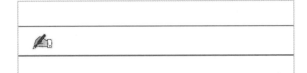

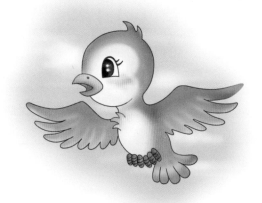

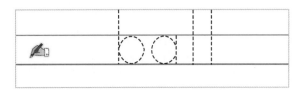
ball

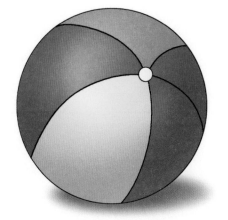

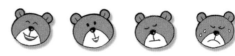

C C

c c

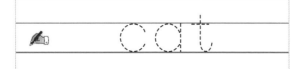
cat

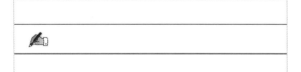
cat

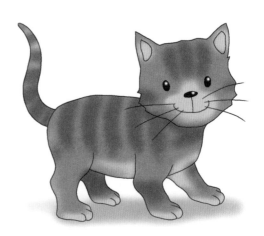

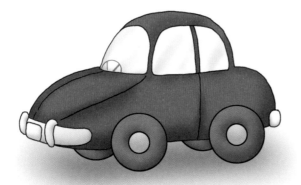

car

car

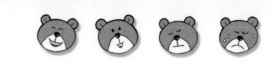

D

d

dog

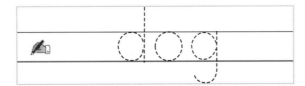

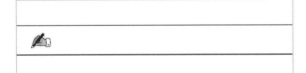

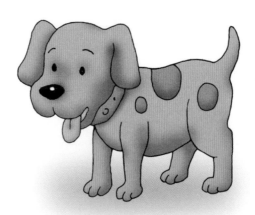

duck

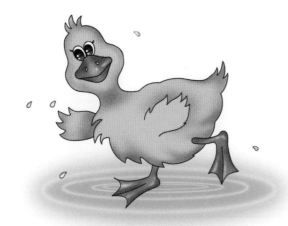

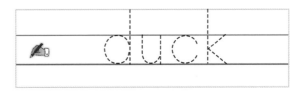

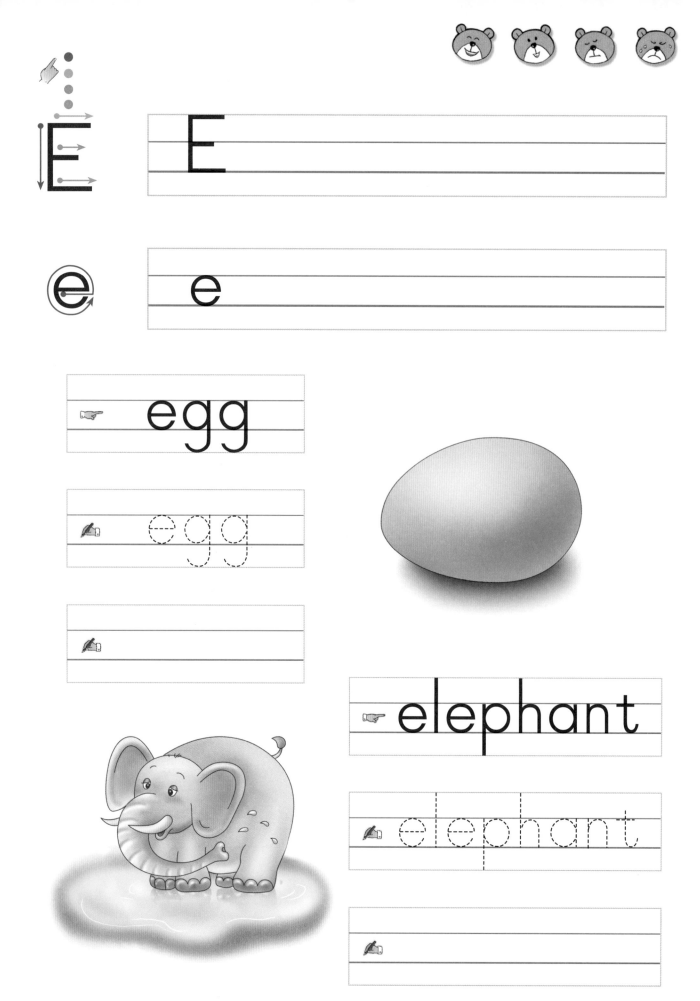

E

e

egg

elephant

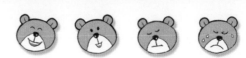

請填上適當的英文字母。

Please fill in the missing letter of each word.

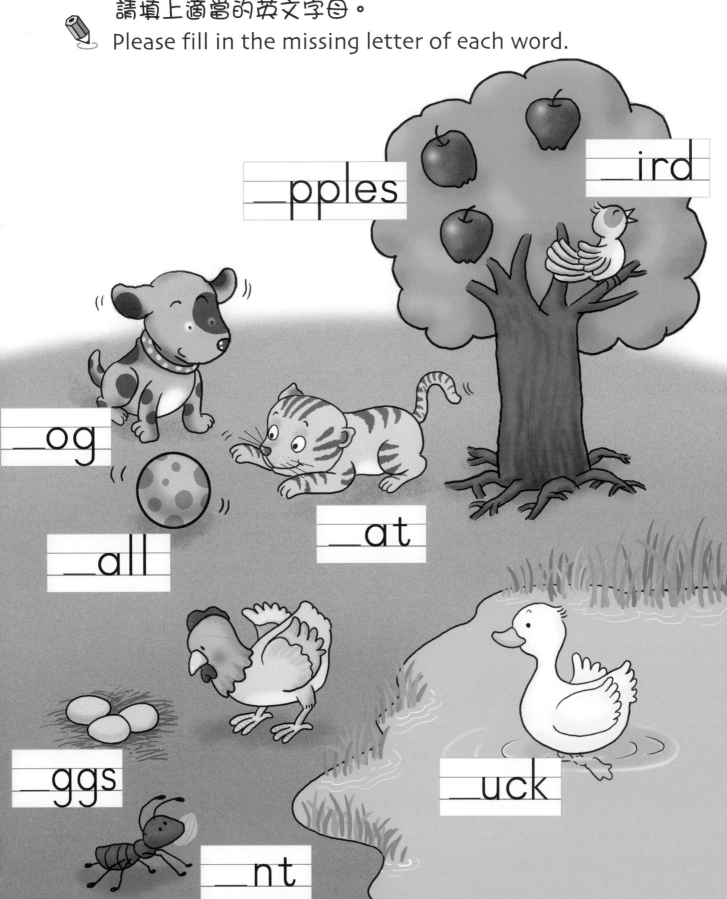

__pples

__ird

__og

__at

__all

__ggs

__uck

__nt

F F

f f

fan

fan

fish

fish

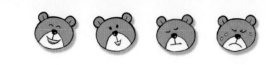

G | G

g | g

girl

girl

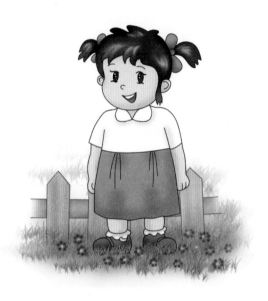

goat

goat

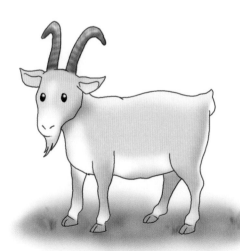

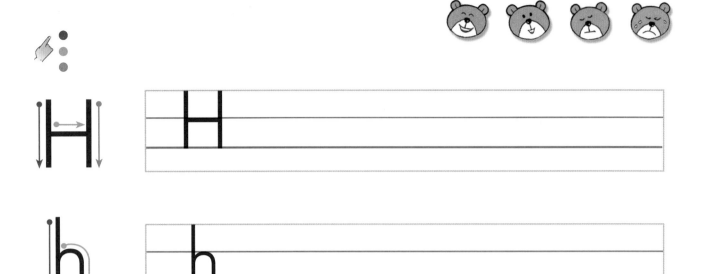

H

h

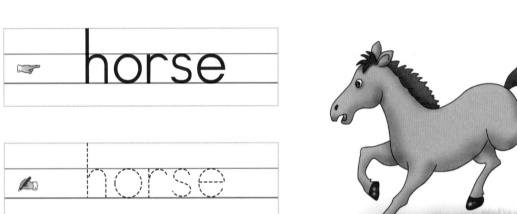

horse

horse

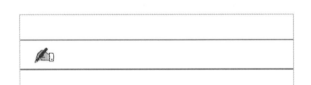

house

house

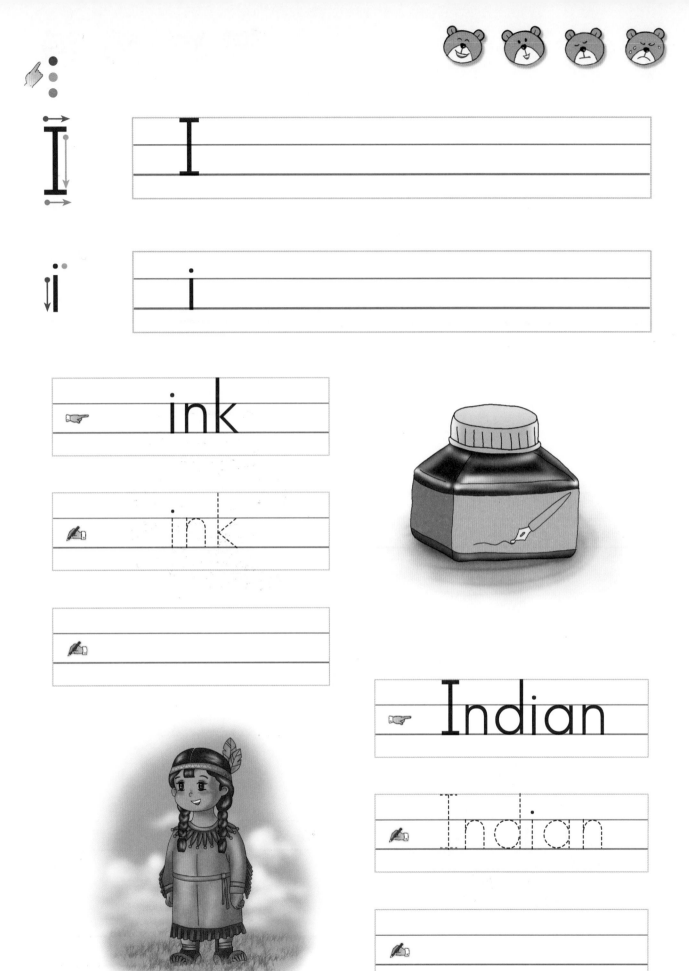

I

i

ink

ink

Indian

Indian

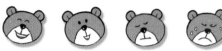

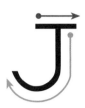

J

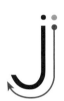

j

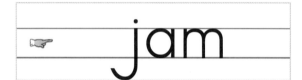

jam

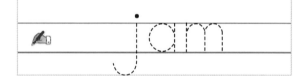

jam

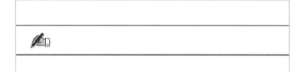

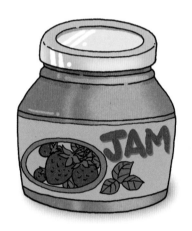

jelly

jelly

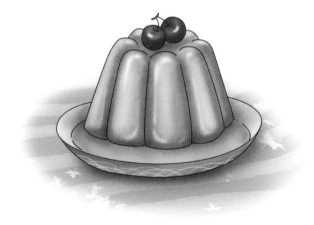

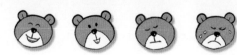

配 對
Matching

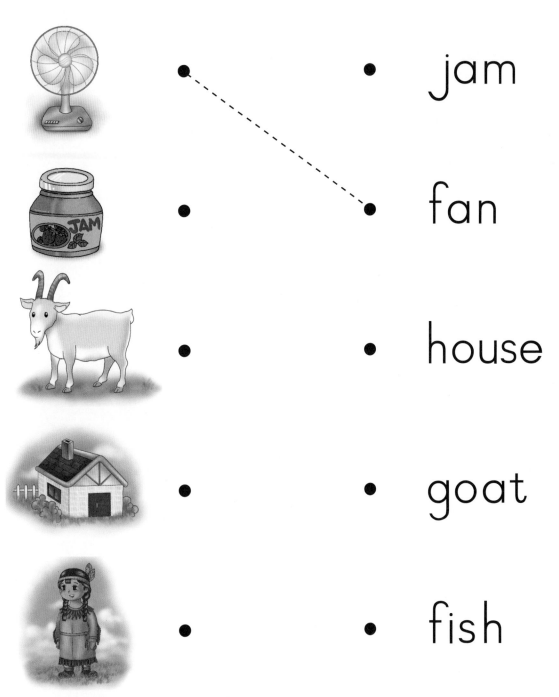

- jam

- fan

- house

- goat

- fish

- Indian

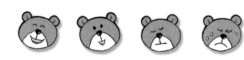

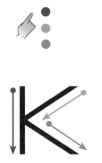

K K

k k

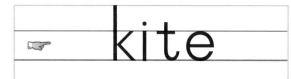

kite

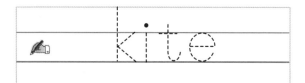

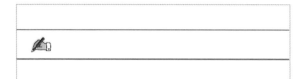

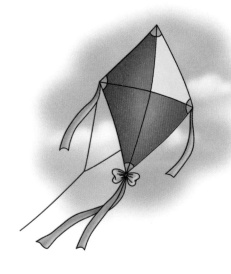

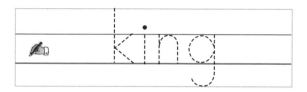

king

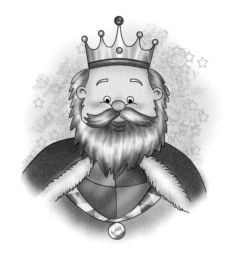

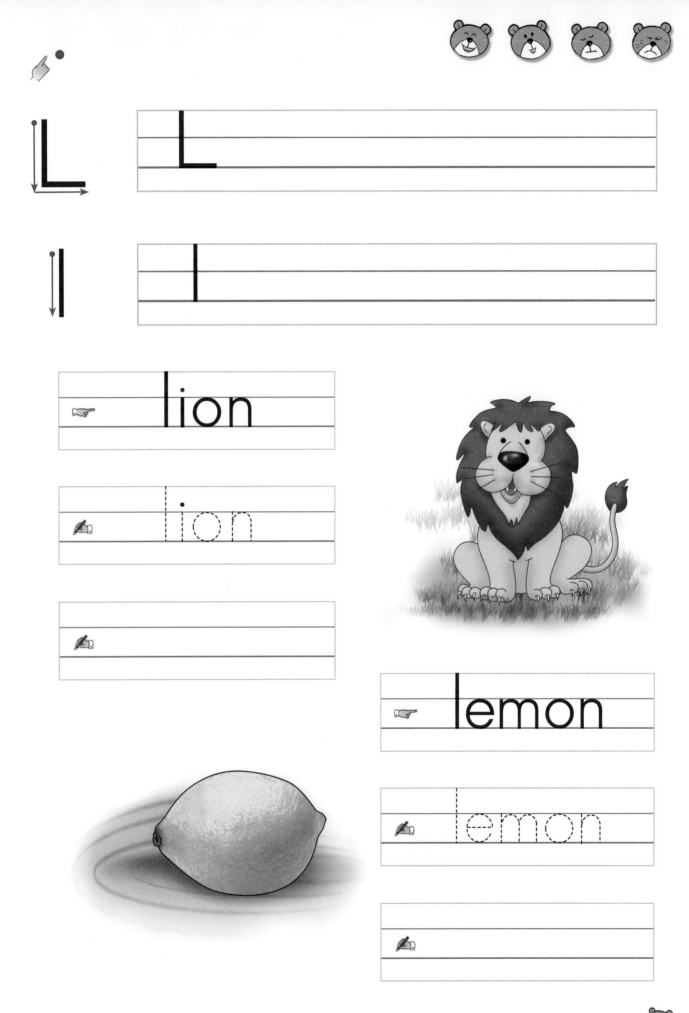

lion

lion

lemon

lemon

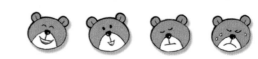

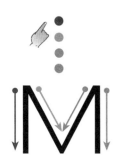

M

m

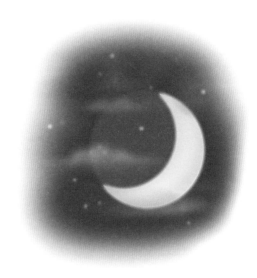

moon

moon

mouse

mouse

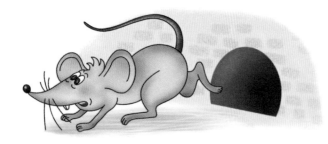

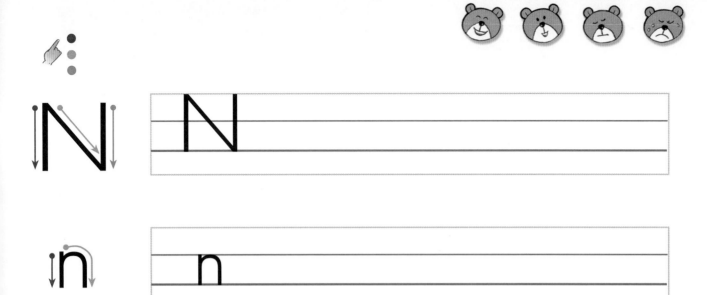

N N

n n

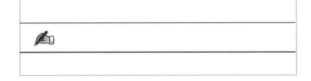
nest

nest

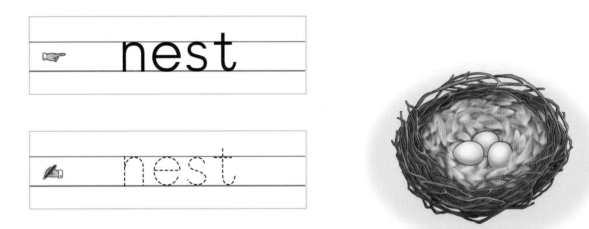

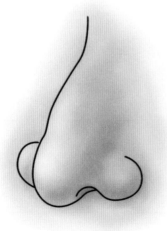

nose

nose

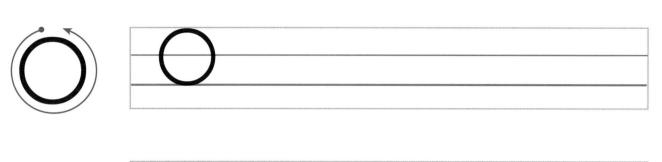

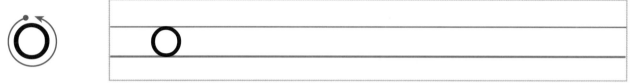

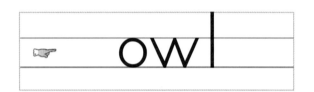

owl

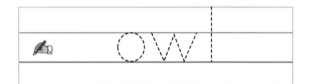

owl

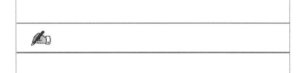

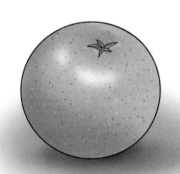

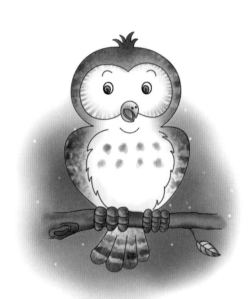

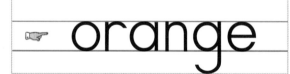

orange

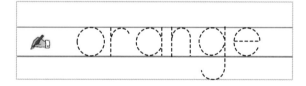

orange

請圈出適當的圖畫。
Please circle the correct pictures.

k			
l			
m			
n			
o			

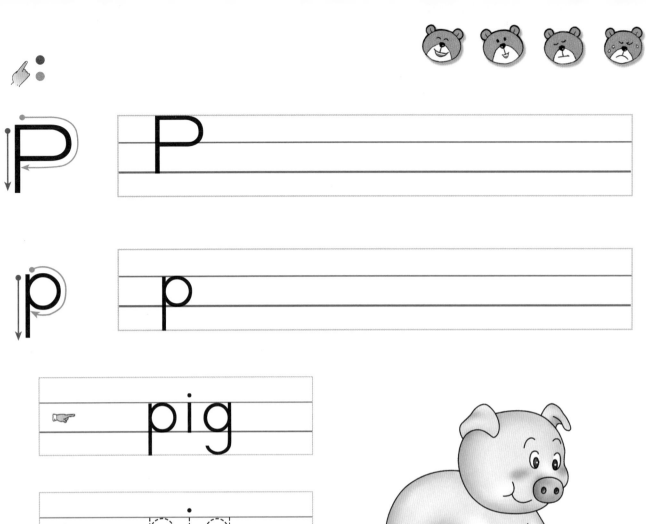

P   P

p   p

pig

pig

pencil

pencil

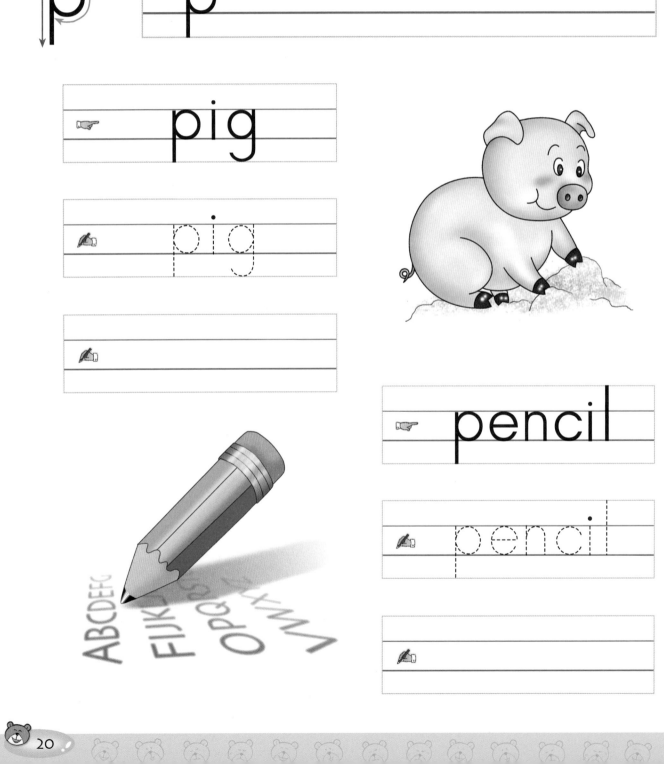

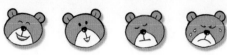

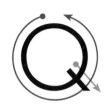

Q

q

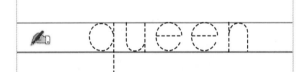
queen

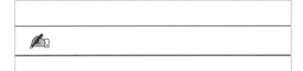
queen

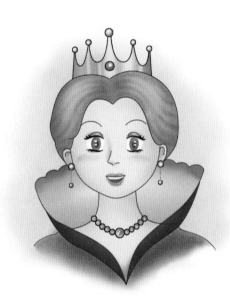

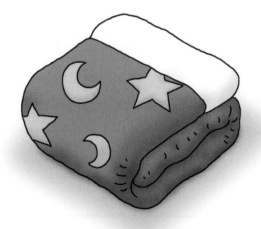

quilt

quilt

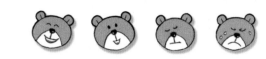

 R

r

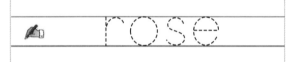 rose

rose

rabbit

rabbit

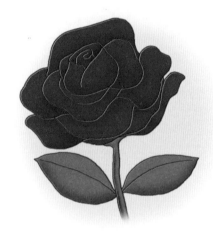

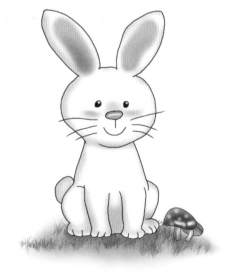

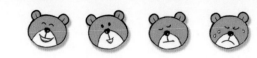

S   S

s   s

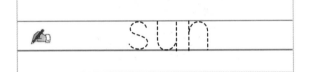
sun

sun

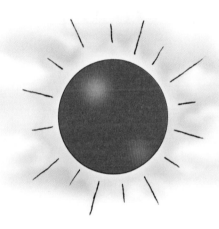

snake

snake

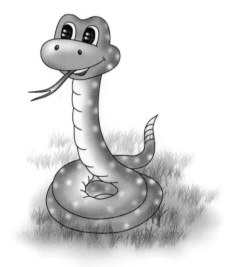

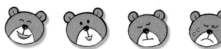

T

t

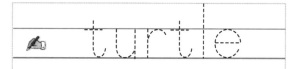
turtle

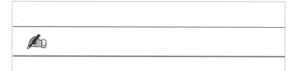
turtle

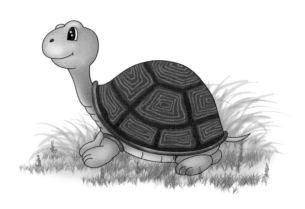
teacher

teacher

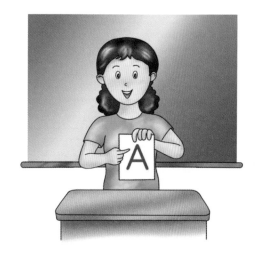

請把適當的圖畫填上顏色。
Please colour the right pictures.

pig	
turtle	
rabbit	
snake	

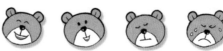

U

u

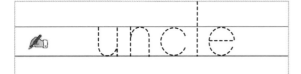

uncle

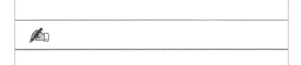

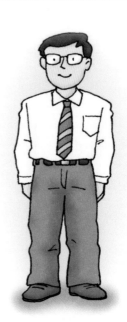

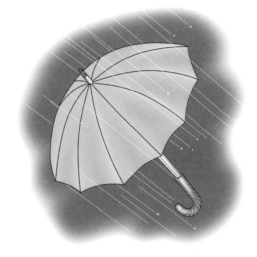

umbrella

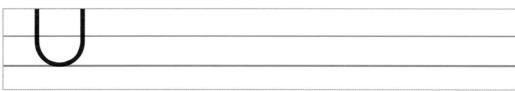

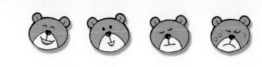

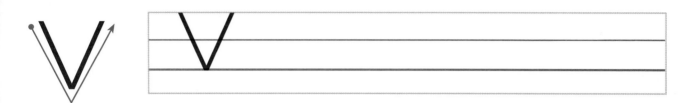

V   V

v   v

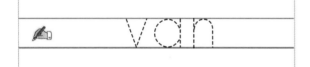
van

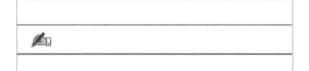
van

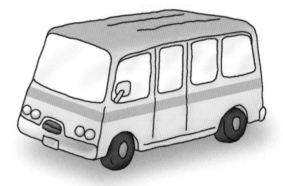

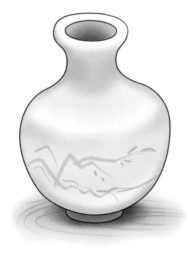

vase

vase

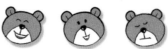

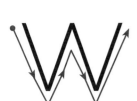

W

W

watch

watch

window

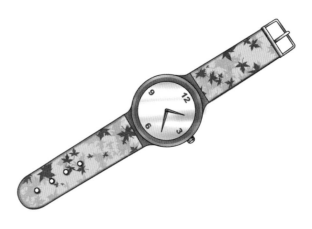

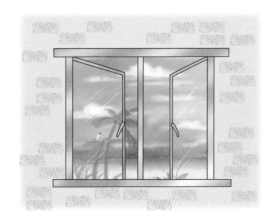

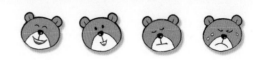

 X

 x

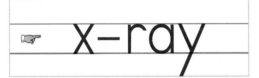

x-ray

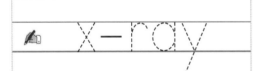

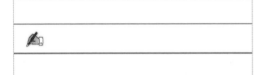

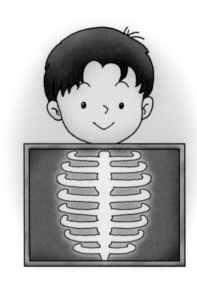

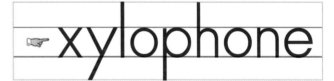

xylophone

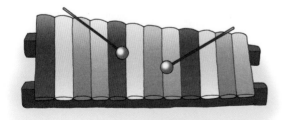

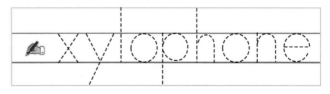

Y

y

yo-yo

yo - yo

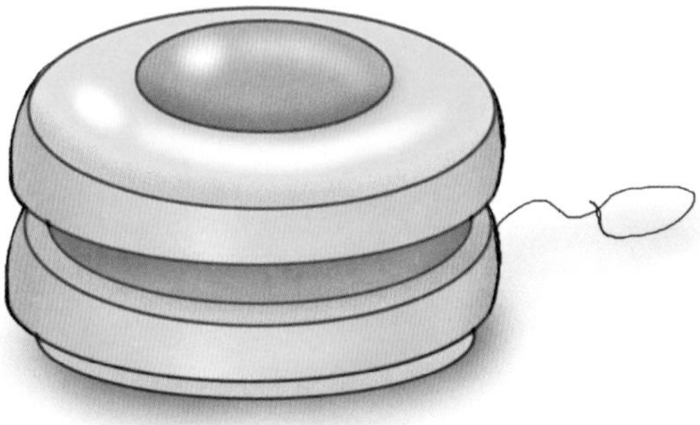

yellow

yellow

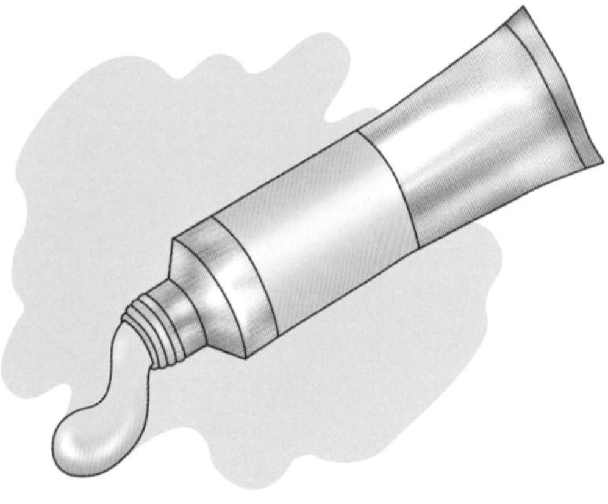

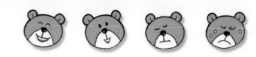

Z   Z

z   z

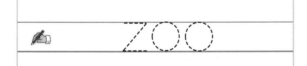
zoo

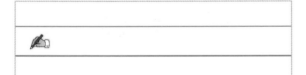
zoo

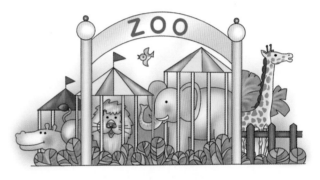

zebra

zebra

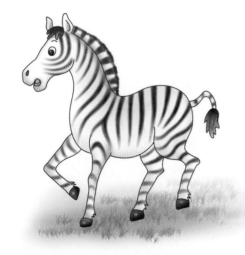

請圈出正確的字。

Please circle the right words.

under   umbrella

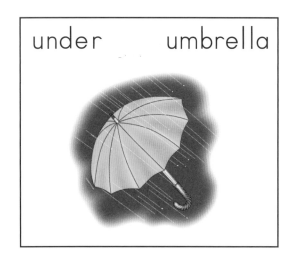

vase   van

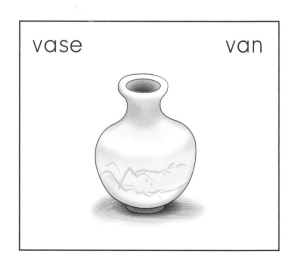

watch   window

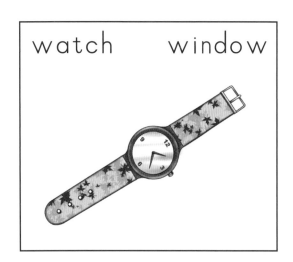

x-ray   xylophone

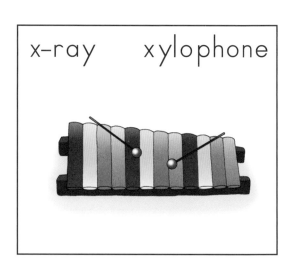

yellow   yo-yo

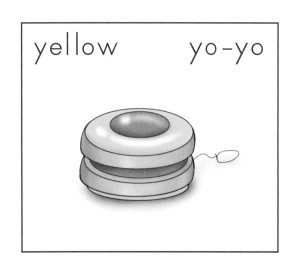

zebra   zoo

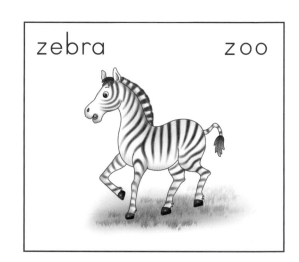